INSPIRE

Poems to Inspire, Reflect, and Stimulate Change

Portia N. Leonard

INSPIRE
POEMS TO INSPIRE, REFLECT, AND STIMULATE CHANGE

Unless otherwise indicated, all scripture quotations are from The Holy Bible, English Standard Version® (ESV®). Copyright ©2001 by Crossway Bibles, a division of Good News Publishers. Used by permission. All rights reserved.

iUniverse books may be ordered through booksellers or by contacting:

iUniverse
1663 Liberty Drive
Bloomington, IN 47403
www.iuniverse.com
1-800-Authors (1-800-288-4677)

Because of the dynamic nature of the Internet, any web addresses or links contained in this book may have changed since publication and may no longer be valid. The views expressed in this work are solely those of the author and do not necessarily reflect the views of the publisher, and the publisher hereby disclaims any responsibility for them.

Any people depicted in stock imagery provided by Getty Images are models, and such images are being used for illustrative purposes only. Certain stock imagery © Getty Images.

ISBN: 978-1-5320-7503-2 (sc)
ISBN: 978-1-5320-7502-5 (e)

Library of Congress Control Number: 2019909246

Print information available on the last page.

iUniverse rev. date: 12/17/2019

To my parents, Neal C. Leonard Sr. and the late Arzelma B. Leonard. Thanks for your love, support, and sacrifice.

Contents

My heart is full of gratitude for my family and friends. I am forever thankful for author Rhontina Lynn Burroughs Dunn's endless encouragement during the final stages of the book. I am blessed to have intercessors the late Mrs. Priscilla Simmons, Rev. Barbara Sands, and Prophetess Janice Butler faithfully pray for me. Also, I would like to thank my Pastor Rev. Dr. Sam Davis for his spiritual leadership, guidance, and encouragement to live in my God-given gifts. If I missed listing your name, please forgive me. Most of all, I thank God for giving me the ability and passion to write a book and the patience to see it though.

Next Time

The next time you visit the baby nursery, say a prayer for the parents whose baby is in the morgue.

As you celebrate Mother's Day, say a prayer for those suffering with infertility or for the mother whose child has been incarcerated or abducted.

When you want to cuss, instead, send up praise.

As you pass judgement on your neighbor, remember that you have a past too.

The next time you are praying, remember those who can't pray for themselves.

Choosing to be silent when you should have spoken, please remember those who have no voice.

Amid discrimination remember those who paid the price for your rights.

The next time you face injustice and don't speak against it, remember those who did and died.

During church service, remember those who can't freely practice their religion.

Just Like That

Life is short. Eat dessert first.

Life is short, so stop and smell the roses.

It's time to value the life God gave us because it can be taken just like that.

Who knew life could be taken away just by crossing the street or chewing on a pork rind?

Can you imagine enjoying a peaceful day just sitting on a front porch and being hit bullet by a stray?

The excitement of spending time with family and friends at a theatre, a game, at a stadium, or sitting in a pew at church, all taken away by a sniper.

Let's value our lives and the lives of others because they can be taken just like that.

Just like that.

Trapped

Trapped in a negative mind-set, I cannot move beyond what is engraved in my mind.

The thoughts of failure are my roadblock.

Arrows of negativity shot like bullets against any positive thoughts.

Past experiences won't allow me to see beyond the failure.

A negative mind-set aborts the vision God gave me.

I must yield to the unknown and walk by faith to fully see what I can do through Christ.

No Means No

I mean what I say, and that is no.

Don't you know the meaning of no?

I said no, but in your mind I mean yes or it's okay.

When I say no, I mean no.

You say, "You mean yes."

I said no.

You say, "Don't you want it?"

I say no.

I mean no.

No means no.

Leaky Vessel

I witness you wearing an orange jumpsuit, shackled like a runaway slave.

My heart pounds as if it's going to burst out of my chest.

My mouth is wide open, but there is no sound because the pain is so deep and I am numb.

My flesh and blood are bound, and I can't help.

I am silent, but my heart is leaking.

I come home to you, and I see your bags packed.

You can't take the pain, so you leave. Now the pain is twice as deep.

Because I am leaking with sorrow and pain, I can't eat or sleep.

Pain and sorrow have numbed my mind.

I cry endlessly day and night.

My words are now moaned and I feel nothing.

I am blind by mixed emotions.

I am trying to move forward, but my feet are too heavy.

I am in a dark place.

I am leaking and I can't find peace.

Help!

I Need Thee

I hear the familiar hymn,

I need thee, Oh I need thee, in my head. *

There is a battle between the spirit and the flesh.

In this battle, my soul is parched like the hot, dry desert, in need of God's living water.

I need God's hand to lead me into the path I so desperately want to follow, but fear grips me tightly.

The flesh is trying to capture the new creature like the Egyptians chased the Israelites.

I desperately need the healing balm of Gilead to heal the aches and pains of life's wounds and afflictions.

Oh, I need thee.

*2018 hymnal.net

Crawl Up and ... Not Die

I want to crawl up but not die.

Perhaps if I crawl up in the fetal position, someone will notice me.

Hopelessness,

Fatigue,

Stress,

Burdens,

In my head, I hear the oh so familiar "crawl up and die," but I dare not say die.

My lips will not utter "crawl up and die."

I don't want to die.

I have too much life.

Today, I feel too much life was snatched out of me, so I want to crawl up but not die.

I am so tired.

This job is not fulfilling anymore.

I feel lost, not appreciated, and taken for granted.

This job today makes me want to crawl up but not die.

Empty

I am amid laughter, joy, and fellowship.
Everyone around me is laughing and enjoying themselves.
I am laughing on the outside, but inside, I am empty.

I am laughing, but it's not from a joyous place.
I desire joy, but what is wrong?
Have I given away too much joy?
I have given so much of myself that I can't find my joy

Free

I just want to be free.
Free from your expectations of me.
Why do you think I should be what you want me to be?
Can't I be free?
Free from others' standards and beliefs?
Free from your expectations and choices.
I just want to be free.
Free to be who God has called me to be.
Free.

Weak

When I am at my weakest,
I am strong.
When I am at my lowest,
You give me a high.
When I am in turmoil,
Your presence brings peace.
When I am on my last dime,
You provide every need.
When I am lonely,
You are my best companion.
Thank you, God.

Than

You must be stronger than your struggle,
Bigger than your problem,
Wiser than your weakest imagination and more determined than procrastination,
Louder than a whisper,
Purer than dirty thoughts,
Friendlier than your enemies,
Sharper than the edge of a sword.

Looking in the Mirror

I see a reflection of myself.
I can see my physical beauty and flaws.
Does my physical beauty outweigh inner beauty?
Does my make up
Mask my insecurity,
Mask my pain,
Mask my lying,
Mask my mental instability?
Looking closer in the mirror,
Can you see God's reflection?
Do you possess his glory?
Does his light radiate in you?

Crooked Crown

Hey, queen,
What's up with that crooked crown?
That ain't the way you suppose to wear it.
What's wrong with cha?
Sumthin' ain't right with the queen.
Has your king left you?
Perhaps you find another woman's or another man's number in his pocket.
Is his mind somewhere else when he is looking straight at cha?
Did your king lie too many times, break promises time after time?
Did your king lose his job?
Another woman at your door saying she is pregnant by your man,
Bills are due and money is short,
Found weed in your son's pocket and birth control in your daughter's purse,
A friend betrayed you.
What's up with that crooked crown?
The Church asking for money you want to give but money is short,
Family sick,
Children sick,
You sick,
Crooked crown

Plastic Doll

I flatten my belly and have breast enhancement.

My lips have fillers, and my hips are lifted and firm.

Flawlessly manicured nails along with the hair that's fried, dyed, and laid to the side,

Teeth capped,

Ears and stomach pierced

I am tucked, tightened, sucked—all for a perfect image.

When the image fades, can you handle

What's real?

Fearfully and Wonderfully Made

As I gaze into the mirror, self-image precedes a flawed image.

I can't see how I am fearfully and wonderfully made, because I am always comparing myself
to an untarnished image.

My eyes only see the flabby arms, thick thighs, dark or pale skin tone, stretchmarks, nappy
hair, and flat butt or anything negative.

This worldly image in my mind portrays an immaculate and untarnished image.

God didn't make us to be flawless.

God said we are fearfully and wonderfully made, with flaws and all.

Are You That Woman?

Are you the woman with an issue of blood?
Are you bossy and evil like Jezebel?
An adored Queen Ester?
Rejected like Leah?
A warrior like Deborah?
Highly favored as Mary, the mother of Jesus?
Loved like Rachel?
Disobedient Queen Vashti,
Or
A deceiver like Delilah?

Friends Girls and Girl Friends

Your most loyal supporters,
The loyal ones,
Your best cheerleaders,
The best confidants,
Ride-or-die chicks
Tell you when you are wrong and when you are right,
Always in your corner,
Friends forever.

Always a Lady

Once upon a time, there were standards to be a lady,
It was a rite of passage.
Ladies were taught standards, but others were not taught at all.
Ladies do this, and others don't do that.
Ladies do not use foul language.
Ladies sit with their legs crossed.
Ladies are not loud.
Ladies are charming and sweet.
Always be a lady.

A Special Woman

Be the kind of woman whose smile radiates instant joy.
Be the kind of woman who will make every woman be a lady,
The woman whose man blushes when others say your name.
Be the woman who gives the shirt off her back because she knows God is her provider.
Be the woman who has walk on water faith.
Be the woman whose prayers reaches heaven gate.
Be the woman who, when she walks in a room, the glory of God fills the room.
Be a special woman.

Be

Be the kind of woman who can stand against the pressure of this world.
Be strong but not broken.
Let's be fearfully and wonderfully made, as God created us to be.
Don't be what others want us to be.
Stand with a man or stand-alone.
Stand for others who can't stand for themselves.
Be God-fearing, desirable, daring, charming, and irresistible.

Bedroom Candy

Be irresistible.
Give him his heart's desire.
Be the delight he can't and won't resist.

Addict

I am addicted to you.

When I am around you, I am on a natural high.

When I am away from you, I have withdrawals.

I sit next to you and get the shakes.

When I know you are coming to see me, I feel anxious.

When you say goodbye, I feel sad.

A Thief in the Night

I am determined, strong, and focused.
You whispered in my ear; then a drastic change entered my mind, so now I can't focus.
I am weak as water, troubled, confused and I have lost my way.
Now,
Since the drastic change, I am totally dependent on you.

A Piece of a Man

I heard through the grapevine it's better to have a piece of man than not have a man at all.

He takes a piece of me; then he leaves to get a piece of his other woman.

After returning from his other woman, he returns to me what another piece she didn't give him.

Truth be told, we only got a piece of him.

We allowed him to give us only a piece of him.

Can I?

Can my fries go with your shake?
Can I speak freely without you judging me?
Can I invite you to my place without you trying to cross the line?
Can I walk down the street with a hoodie?
Can I wear ruby red lipstick and you not judge me?
Can I have food stamps in a Gucci bag?
Can I drive a Lexus and live in a hotel?
Can I smoke weed and not be judged?
Can I get on the elevator without you clenching your purse?
Can I?

A Woman's View

Looking at you from across a jail cell,

I still see you free.

Witnessing you in handcuffs,

I see the potential.

Holding you while your body shakes from drug withdrawal,

I still see you clean.

Reading your report card, filled with Fs,

I still see you as an achiever.

Wiping your bloody nose from a fistfight,

I see you as a fighter.

From a woman's view,

We see beyond the circumstances and see the potential.

Connections

As a giver of life, beware of your connections.

A woman produces life.

If you connect with death, it will take your life.

A connection with a liar will take your truth.

If you connect with a loser, eventually, you may lose your way.

Connections with a cheater will cheat you out of trust, confidence, and self-value.

Hope

I want to believe.
She wants to believe.
We want to believe that prince charming is out there somewhere.

I want to be believe.
She wants to believe.
We want to believe true love waits.

I want to believe.
She wants to believe.
We want to believe he will be all we hoped for.

I want to believe.
She wants to believe.
We want to believe.
Our waiting has not been in vain.

I want to believe.
She wants to believe.
We want to believe.

Simple Things

It's the simple things you do.

A phone call just to say you were thinking of me.

A single rose left on my pillow or a gentle kiss on the neck.

You slowly wrapping your hands around my waist.

A whisper of "I love you" in the middle of the night.

A stare that tells me "You so sexy."

Your hand on my shoulder for support when I am feeling low.

Massaging my feet after a long day,

Leaving a sweet note in my lunchbox in the morning.

When I am sad, you hold me tight.

The two of us on a picnic blanket, gazing at the stars or sharing an ice cream sundae at our
   favorite place.

You washing the dishes after I cook

Or

You washing my hair when I don't feel like it.

Cruising on a cool afternoon in your sports coupe,

My head on your shoulder after a long day.

It's the simple things.

To Love Again

Will I trust my heart to love again?

After all, it was scattered to pieces, and now I am whole.

Will I allow myself to let go of the past and experience love?

Will I risk it all and allow another man to enter my secret space?

I often wonder if I can share love again like before, or have better.

Can I take the chance to love again?

Lady Parts

The delightful, delicate, intricate parts of a woman, which connect to her inner emotions, and
the soul of the one she encounters.
It's not a place for invasion.
It's her private space where she becomes most vulnerable.

You + Me

Take my hand and lead me under the sunset.

Let's feel the soft rays of the morning sun and listen quietly to the chirping of birds.

Take my hand and lead me to a path of lovers' bliss to encounter pure intimacy with just a
gentle kiss.

Let's walk hand in hand and let our love flow like ocean waves.

As we sit side by side, we can feel the pure joy of being.

Let's gaze into the sky and see ourselves loving each other endlessly, as the sky above.

You + Me = Ecstasy

Caress me with your words.
Speak sweet words to my heart.
Arouse my senses with the gentle touch of your hand down my back.
Run your fingers through my hair to awaken my senses.
Come close to me so I can feel our hearts beat in rhythm.
Stimulate my mind with your sweet words I love to hear.
Kiss me gently and slowly under the crescent moon.

Ying N Yang

I dated yum yum and played around with dumb dumb.

Dumb dumb had swagger and yum yum had clout.

I yearned for yum yum and dumb dumb.

There was adventure with dumb dumb but rules to follow with yum yum.

Both yum yum and dumb dumb were needy.

Their need for affirmation and love overwhelmed me.

If you give totally to someone who is not your mate, then what is left to give the mate God has
given you?

Your Love Cuts Like a Knife

The words you say to me cut like a knife instead of comforting me.

The hands that should hold me bruise me.

My thoughts of you should be loving; instead, my mind is filled with fear.

Your feet should lead me on a path to success; instead, you kick me with them.

I should stand beside you; instead, my side is bruised with your punches.

Your love hurts me.

What Cha Call Me?

Queen

Princess

Natural beauty

Mother of civilization

Strong

Virtuous

wrench

h ... (garden tool)

side piece

homewrecker

lazy

scandalous

hateful

angry

loud

Strong willed

Proud

Educated

Warrior

Loving
Caring
Fine
Supportive
Boss

Who Am I to You?

Am I your support system?

Am I your friend or lover?

Am I your problem solver and heart fixer?

Am I your mama or sister?

Am I your cover-up, side piece, or your fix in the time of need?

Am I your counselor or teacher?

Am I your prayer partner?

Who am I to you?

Stand

If I lost my CEO position, filed for bankruptcy, lost all of my worldly possessions, would you still love me?

Perhaps an unexpected health crisis brings me to a medical emergency, I can't work. Will you stick by my side?

If I were sex-addicted, drug-addicted, food-addicted, or a frequent gambler, would you stand to take a chance with me?

Can our love stand?

She/Rib

God made me a woman.
I was created by God and shaped from a man's rib.
I am a support system to help you breathe.
I was not made to be
Traumatized,
Humiliated,
Or abused.

For You

Created to be the opposite of man,

My hair is softer, for you to run your fingers through it.

My skin is softer, so your rough hands can stimulate your emotions.

Hands gentle to touch so you understand when the roughness of life weighs you down,

A gentle touch to calm and relieve the pressure,

My womb to carry your seed and bring forth life,

A life we create together,

I am your rib,

Created to be by your side to support you and help you breathe.

Hidden Treasure

Until he finds me, I will not yield to desperation.
I want allow myself to have false hope.
Idleness will not be a part of my life.
I will keep my heart free from jealousy and bitterness.
Instead, I live each day with a thankful heart.
I will be happy.

Selfish Dog

We crossed paths at an unusual place.

You are the same old person, but you can't see I have changed.

I want you to leave me alone, but you are persistent to continue the conversation.

I am not interested, because you are still talking the same noise as before.

Your mind is still stuck in what we used to be.

I hear you saying you are a changed man, but still saying the same old thing.

I am not who I was when I was with you.

Can't you see I am free from you?

You want what you want what you want to be selfish,

You want me because you are not free and broken.

I see you are still selfish because you only want me for what I can give you.

You don't have nothing to give.

Help for the Needy

As women, it's time to stop allowing the enemy to steal, kill, and destroy.

It's time to stop allowing folks to abuse our children.

It's time to pray for broken marriages.

It's time to pray for generational curses to be broken.

It's time to reach back, reach up, reach down,

To help the drug-addicted mother, sister, daughter, or aunt.

Pray for the abused wife and prostitute and assist the teenage mother.

It's time to take back and look back whence we come,

Big Momma did it, broken and all.

She did it!

Big Momma

She is a living history book.
Experience has taught her well.
Her heart is filled with pure gold.
She has many stories to tell.
Those soft, wrinkled hands are strong.
Those hands cooked many meals,
Scrubbed floors,
Paid college tuition, and
They prayed many a night.

Woman of God

God is my strength, so I seek him early before the dawn of day.

My heart is filled with adoration to him.

When I open my mouth, songs of praise overflow like a flood,

I seek his wisdom to direct my day.

Because prayer is my weapon, I humbly kneel down in his presence.

When I am in his presence, he reconnects me to my life's purpose.

He only is the one who truly understands my needs and comforts me in my deepest pain.

Daily he blesses me with benefits.

I am a woman of God.

I stand before you in awe because of who you are.

I give adoration to you, for you are Abba Father.

You are dear to my heart because you have carefully watched and protected me like a loving father.

I stand with a grateful heart, knowing I am unworthy of your righteousness, and that I am saved by your amazing grace.

I am standing because you stood beside me when I was

Lonely and rejected,

Naked and flawed,

Dirty and ashamed,

Sick and tired.

Today, I stand with unshakeable faith. Daily I will praise and give adoration to God because I am a transformed woman of God.

It's a Good Day

My day started with thinking about daily tasks, etc.—checking emails, planner, fix lunches,
   what to wear.

I grumbled because I felt so overwhelmed.

I needed to enter a quiet place to hear God's voice.

Once in the quiet place, the Lord spoke to me and said, "This is the Lord's day. Rejoice and
   be glad in it".

Then,

I had a different perspective of my day.

I felt refreshed with a positive mind-set.

Victory was in my mind today, and I knew today was a good day.

*The Holy Bible English Standard Version (ESV) Text Edition, 2016. Copyright 2001 by
   Crossway Bibles, a publishing ministry of Good News Publishers.

Dem Country Boys

Dem country boys like fightin' gators,

Eating fried potatoes and sometimes green tomatoes.

They like riding dirt bikes.

They know how to hold you tight in the midnight.

Country slang is their game.

Their love will drive you insane.

They like driving Cadillacs and will give you their shirts off their backs.

They wear boots in winter,

Want to eat something fried for dinner,

Pray for you if you are a sinner,

Hunting,

Fishing,

Grilling,

Shooting,

Bike riding,

Dem country boys.

And the Winner Is …

The winner of the Golden Globe is the woman who had to play several roles in the lives of many people.

The Oscar goes to the woman who performs her daily duties with excellence—mom, wife, sister, teacher, maid, chef, direction, preacher, counselor, etc.

The Nobel Peace Prize goes to the woman who carries the mantel of peace. Peace in her job, home, etc.

The winner of the Mark Twain Prize for American Humor, is the mom who creates endless laughter for her children.

Overflow

My cup is running over.

The blessings in my cup are running over.

The blessings are flowing over hills and valleys.

Temptation put a hole in my cup.

Sin stopped it up.

Jesus blood covered the cup.

God blew on the cup.

Confession mended the cup.

The Holy Spirit revived the cup.

Now my cup continues to run over with blessings.

The Power of a Dollar

Someone sold their body for a dollar, and someone else regrets what they did for a dollar.

Sometimes spouses leave their partners because the one they are cheating with has more dollars.

It's been told a woman or a man may have abandoned their children to get a dollar.

Friends sometimes fight over a dollar, and friendships often are destroyed because of the lack of a dollar.

Hope lost because all hope was in the dollar.

A child was given to a drug dealer in exchange for a dollar.

Babies conceived in a tube because a scientist was provided a dollar.

A life lost because of a dollar.

The power of a dollar.

With a Kiss

I saw lovers embracing each other with a kiss in the park.

At a wedding, I saw a groom salute his bride with a kiss.

At the airport, a soldier passionately embraced his wife with a kiss.

I saw a mother greet her kids after a long school day with a kiss.

A dog at the park licked his friend with a kiss.

I saw a little girl show affection with her doll with a kiss.

Judas identified Jesus with a kiss.

Reflection

Looking back at our relationship, I think I was a fool.

Did I leave because I didn't like who I was becoming?

When I glanced in the mirror, I didn't like the image.

Did I only see you because I allowed you to consume every part of me until I could only see you?

Was I dumb to allow you to play mind games?

Was I all you needed or what you needed at the moment?

Was I a fool or just in love?

Love is blind.

It's time to break the glass.

Dirty Mattress

Just sitting on the edge of this dirty mattress, thoughts of lying on it dare not cross my mind.

Sitting on the edge and wondering why am I back here?

God delivered me from this place, so I never wanted to return.

Here I return sitting on the edge of a dirty mattress with a conscious of what is unclean.

My mind wondering why was I bound by such a fifth in the past.

I let my guard down slightly and moved closer to him.

He began to seduce and touch me.

His words became tantalizing, poisonous, and savage.

His words controlled my mind, with what he said he can do to my body.

I began to pray silently because of my flesh guiding me back to the unclean place.

My body said, "you need this", but the Holy Spirit said, "the consequences would be too great".

Not only did he want my body,

He wanted my virtue.

Printed in the United States
By Bookmasters